Succeed at the CSA

Pass the MRCGP first time - a unifying communication and practical skills guide

Succeed at the CSA

Pass the MRCGP first time – a unifying communication and practical skills guide

3rd Edition

Dr Daniel Berkeley

Succeed at the CSA

Pass the MRCGP first time – a unifying communication and practical skills guide

Copyright: Dr Daniel Berkeley

Published: 27th November 2016

The right of Dr Daniel James Gordon Berkeley to be identified as author of this Work has been asserted by him in accordance with sections 77 and 78 of the Copyright, Designs and Patents Act 1988.

All rights reserved. No part of this publication may be reproduced, stored in retrieval system, copied in any form or by any means, electronic, mechanical, photocopying, recording or otherwise transmitted without written permission from the publisher. You must not circulate this book in any format.

Contents:

An Overview of the CSA and how to pass it
        i. Data gathering, a brief overview
        ii. Management, a brief overview

Communication Skills
        i. Openings
        ii. Rapport
        iii. ICE and how to use it
        iv. How to use summarising
        v. The meeting of two experts
        vi. Making a plan 'truly shared'
        vii. Admitting that you don't know what is going on
        viii. What is really a 'safety net?'
        ix. Running out of time
        x. Complaint
        xi. Bad news
        xii. Telephone consultation
        xiii. Home visit
        xiv. Third party consultation
        xv. Learning difficulties
        xvi. Paediatrics
        xvii. Psychiatric case

Practicalities of the CSA
        i. The run up to the exam
        ii. Keeping a clear mind
        iii. Travel
        iv. The day itself

References

About the Author

For the GP Partners: Doctors, businesspeople, leaders. May this generation not be the last.

Introduction:

First of all, it is extremely important to explain what this book is, and most essentially—what it isn't.

This book is not full of clinical presentations with lists of what to do in 'situation A or B'. It is not full of cases to role play with your colleagues, (although this is very useful, and there are good books on sale that are nicely full of such cases). It is instead an exposition of a 'unifying style of consultation', that you can apply to almost any situation. My aim is not to present to you a proforma that you should follow slavishly, it is instead to help you achieve the ability to think on your feet, and respond in the way the examiners want to an evolving situation. It is to help your interactions with patients move onto the next level. It is a consultation skills book, but one designed specifically for this exam. My aim is to help you pass the exam first time, but then take the skills you have learnt and find you can apply them usefully throughout the rest of your career.

There is a chapter on specific situations as well—consultations which are perhaps a little rarer in real life but yet crop up regularly in the CSA. We will cover these in some special detail later in the book.

And finally, since many people, like me, find being prepared makes them less stressed and therefore more likely to pass the exam. I have also included a final chapter on 'practicalities'. This covers what to expect on the day in terms of timings and the actual running of the exam, and also discusses general strategies to improve your preparation for the exam.

So to sum up, throughout the following chapters I am going to try to show you how you can deal with anything that comes in through the door. I am going to show you that you can consult naturally even though you are about to be put into an extremely unnatural situation—consulting an actor whilst being watched by an examiner in a strange room in London. I am going to show you that you can develop a toolkit of skills that can be used in different situations, skills that CSA examiners love—skills that will score you marks. I am going to try to show you that even if you don't think communication skills are 'your thing', that first, they probably actually are and secondly that you can learn them, use them brilliantly, enjoy using them, and find they not only make your consultations more rewarding but faster too.[1]

I don't think you want to read a large amount about me when you want to be getting on with the serious business of attempting to take what is likely to be the hardest exam you will ever take, but in the interests of showing some qualification to write this book I will briefly introduce myself.

I am in my early thirties and a GP at the practice in Maryport, on the edge of the Lake District and Cumbrian coast. I took and passed the CSA first time in November 2012, whilst not in a GP post, and six months earlier than is usual in our area, right at the start of the ST3 year. To achieve this we worked in a small study group regularly practicing cases and devising new methods and consultation 'tools'. Despite the disadvantages of taking the exam 'too early', all but one of our group of eight passed. My aim is to pass on to you the knowledge and skills that we learnt so that you can have similar success. Subsequently I have gone on to run CSA training sessions for our local GP scheme, as well as speaking at our local trainers' conference on the subject.

In terms of my qualification in terms of writing and media: I am BBC radio Cumbria's resident radio doctor, as well as being the author of the Amazon top 10 action and adventure novels—'Sacramentum', 'Impietas', and 'Ultionis'. This is my first nonfiction book.

An Overview of the CSA and How to pass it

Introduction:

The CSA is marked over three domains, essentially these are data gathering (which includes your ability to examine), management (which includes your ability to explain conditions and treatment options), and communication skills. Time will be spent on all three, but most of this book is devoted to the third section, communication skills.

This is not an attempt to keep the cost of the book down for you by saving paper! In fact there are two good reasons why I have devoted most of these pages to CSA focused communication skills. Firstly, because you can almost certainly do the first two domains: data gathering, and management, very well anyway. As a GP you will have needed to tweak them significantly compared to how you practiced them as a hospital doctor, but any problems you feel you have in them are most likely to be, in actual fact, related to a problem you may have in the third domain—communication skills.

The second reason for focusing on communication skills over the other two domains is that you cannot really score marks in data gathering or management skills unless your communication skills are good. This does seem odd because the three domains are marked separately, but almost all of the 'negative descriptors' listed on the RCGP website, and used to determine your marks, either relate to communication skills directly, or require excellent communication skills to achieve.

Therefore if we can improve communication skills, and also develop *consultation skills*—your ability to run a doctor led, patient centred consultation—we can score higher marks in all three domains.

I have listed the sixteen negative descriptors below, so that you can see for yourself that almost all of them have a significant communication skills/consultation skills theme to them. Therefore it makes sense to spend most of your time working on these skills. Just to make this very clear now: **I am not saying that you do not need knowledge to pass the CSA.** Of course you do. But please do not spend all your CSA revision reading NICE guidelines. This is a communication and consultation skills test first, and a knowledge test a very distant second.

The sixteen negative descriptors[2]:

1. Disorganised / unstructured consultation

2. Does not recognise the issues or priorities in the consultation (for example, the patient's problem, ethical dilemma etc)

3. Shows poor time management

4. Does not identify abnormal findings or results or fails to recognise their implications

5. Does not undertake physical examination competently, or use instruments proficiently

6. Does not make the correct working diagnosis or identify an appropriate range of differential possibilities

7. Does not develop a management plan (including prescribing and referral) reflecting knowledge of current best practice

8. Does not show appropriate use of resources, including aspects of budgetary governance

9. Does not make adequate arrangements for follow-up and safety netting

10. Does not demonstrate an awareness of management of risk or make the patient aware of relative risks of different options

11. Does not attempt to promote good health at opportune times in the consultation

12. Does not appear to develop rapport or show awareness of patient's agenda, health beliefs and preferences

13. Poor active listening skills and use of cues. Consulting may appear formulaic (slavishly following a model and/or unresponsive to the patient), and lacks fluency

14. Does not identify or use appropriate psychological or social information to place the problem in context

15. Does not develop a shared management plan, demonstrating an ability to work in partnership with the patient

16. Does not use language and/or explanations that are relevant and understandable to the patient

Data Gathering, a brief overview:

'First principles, Clarice. Simplicity. Read Marcus Aurelius. Of each particular thing ask: what is it in itself? What is its nature?'

Hannibal Lecter, The Silence of the Lambs

You only have ten minutes. Don't waste them. Ideally you want to spend no more than around six minutes of the ten available to you taking the history and doing the examination. If you don't already practice in this way it will feel like almost no time at all, so you need to stay extremely focused, and you need to practice to get good at it—like any skill.

Try to start with open questions. Avoid clichés though such as: 'OK, can you tell me more about that', as a response to the patient's presenting complaint. The actor will very likely say something like: 'what do you want to know?', which is a bit off-putting.

Patients in the exam will not always behave like patients in real life. Our general experience as a group having taken the exam, was that the patients were keen to follow their script as much as possible, and on the whole seemed to expect focused questions early. They seemed uncomfortable with the extremely open questions that we tend to use in real life. This is to be expected and makes sense, the patient actor doesn't really have the illness, and they only have a partial back-story. By their very nature therefore they will have less to elaborate on than a real person with a real problem. Perhaps pre-empt this issue by asking a less general, but still open question. If possible base your questions on something the patient has already said so that there is a link, this makes things flow well and looks great. In real life it is also fantastic for developing rapport as the patient is shown that you are listening from the outset.

e.g. *'you mentioned that your head has been hurting a lot recently, and that's why you have come here today, could you tell me how this all started?'*

You want to ask about Ideas, Concerns and Expectations early, perhaps in your first questions if you are feeling bold. There is a lot more about this in the communication skills chapter and there are specific ways you can ask them that make them seem less formulaic and more useful.

Many of the cases in the CSA have a strong social, particularly occupational, slant to them. It's worth asking about this directly if it's not immediately offered to you by the patient.

e.g. *'so you've been suffering from back pain for a few days, do you mind if I ask if it's been causing you any difficulties at work at all?'*

You may find that the patient's occupation is given in the notes you have for them. If so, it's highly likely to be relevant, try to think how it could affect the consultation before the patient comes in so that you are prepared.

You may, after asking a few open questions, determining ICE, and discovering about impact of the condition, need to ask a few more questions to really nail down the diagnosis and particularly to exclude specific red flags. It's perfectly reasonable given the time constraints of the CSA (and real life consulting of course) to do this in quite a closed fashion. If you are going to do this, and I recommend that you try it, it's extremely important that you *signpost* what you are going to do. If you don't signpost it then it is highly likely that the patient will recoil from this type of interrogation. When asking about red flags in this way you might also need to specifically signpost that some of what you are asking may sound scary or odd.

e.g. *'OK, I've got a pretty good idea what is going on here, but there are a few important **medical type questions** I need to ask you, just to rule out anything more serious, is that OK?*
Have you lost any weight recently?
Have you noticed any shortness of breath?
Has the pain ever woken you from sleep?
This last one might be a bit personal, I hope that is OK. Have you noticed any bleeding from your back passage at all?'

Again just an example, but hopefully this illustrates the idea well. This technique can save you minutes, and not affect your rapport as long as you do it with signposting and do it at the very end of history taking when you are about to move on to examination or management. You could also quickly enquire as to whether the patient is on any meds you don't know about, and also enquire about allergies, alcohol, smoking, and recreational drugs at this point, if this seems relevant to the case.

You *may* now need to do an examination. I say may because please don't do one if you wouldn't in real life. You won't need to actually physically perform an examination in most of the cases, perhaps just in one or two. Unless actually witnessing the examination and marking it is part of that case the examiner will usually either tell you it was normal before you do it, or pass you a card with the findings on.

It's important to remember that the examiner won't stop you until you are literally about to do the examination. So do just as you would normally, explain what you want to examine, why, and then start to perform the examination. If you are allowed to continue then do so, it is probably being marked.

Remember that the cases are designed to be completed in ten minutes and are written by GPs. They are not expecting an MRCP examination, in fact you would probably lose marks for doing this as it would be 'poor time management'. Do a very focused examination, just like you would do in real life. Don't feel you have to offer an examination in every case. If you would not examine in real life, why offer to do so now? Also do not be tempted to reel off a list of examinations you want to do in the hope of seeming thorough. What if they asked you to do them all? Examine in the same focused way that you take your history—make every single thing you do count. You only have ten minutes.

Management a brief overview:

'You've got to have a system!'

Harry Hill

So you have taken the most focused history you can, and perhaps done a brief, focused, and relevant examination. You have now got around four minutes left (hopefully). You think you know what is wrong and you have a plan. You also should have some idea of what the patient thought was wrong, and what *they* want you to do about it.

So all you have to do is try to join these two agendas together...

This of course can be a challenge, and it is this facet of your consultation that is mainly being tested in this section of the exam. In essence a consultation is the GP with his agenda, and the patient with their agenda, trying to find safe and mutually acceptable middle ground. This is the part of the case where you need to demonstrate the skills required to negotiate this to the examiner.

A useful technique can be to try to use their ideas, concerns, and expectations, in your explanation. This shows that you have been listening, and makes it easier to negotiate a plan.

e.g. *'OK, so you came with these headaches and you have been worried that they could be something serious, specifically some type of brain tumour. And you were hoping that we might refer you to see a neurologist at the hospital. Well the good news is that my examination of your eyes and nerves of the face was completely normal. This doesn't rule out cancer, but it does make it less likely. The really good news though is that the story you gave me about the symptoms doesn't really point towards cancer either, in fact it points to quite a common problem called 'tension headache'. Thankfully this is something we can help you with. How do you feel about that?'*

It's really important to let the patient speak as much as you can. Here you have given them a way of joining up your agenda: (not referring, and discussing analgesia and stress reduction), with theirs: (urgent referral). You need to see how they respond, and take it from there.

You might then want to offer an explanation about tension headache.

e.g. *'So would you like to know a bit more about these so called 'tension headaches'?*

The patient may want this, or perhaps they have been briefed to save you time at this point, and will just want to know what you can do to help.

When you are discussing management, you want to try to offer the patient some options rather than dictate what must be done. But you must remember that just because the consultation is patient *centred*, does not mean it has to also be patient *led*. Just in the same way that you cannot allow the patient to spend six minutes telling you irrelevant information about their pets whilst history taking, you also cannot start to offer options which are poor management.

It's very likely that some of your CSA cases will be testing how you deal with a patient that wants you to agree to a management option which is unreasonable or unsafe. If this happens you need to explore why they want this course of action and explain why that might not be the best option. You could then go on to discuss how some other options might be better. You cannot always do what the patient wants; this is OK, and to simply do what the patient wants every time will not net you good marks in the exam (nor be safe in real life either!).

Try to do a brief summary of treatment options, always including what the patient can do to help themselves. Then try to explain the pros and cons of the different options. Keep 'chunking and checking'. In practice this means checking understanding and asking what the patient thinks about an option that you have told them about. This will help close off avenues the patient is not interested in, saving you minutes of unnecessary explanation. Try to stay positive as far as possible, emphasising what you and the patient can do to improve the situation.

e.g. *'the good news is.... this tends to get better in time/we have a tablet that can help/this is not a life threatening illness'* etc.

If you are running out of time try to get safety netting in quickly, even if you haven't completely finished explaining management options. As soon as the bell goes the patient leaves and you will get no marks for safety netting if you've not done any. It's really important so try to include it throughout the consultation.

The communication chapters that follow describe most of the techniques touched on above in much greater detail. But in summary you could look at the bare bones of a consultation like this:

Summary framework for a CSA consultation:

Say hello, consider shaking hands

Get presenting complaint

Open questions including ICE, effect on life

Focused closed questions with signposting, red flags, drugs, allergies

Examination (if needed)

(6 minutes approximately are up)

Explanation and discussion of agendas to find a 'middle path'

Management (shared options)

Safety netting

Shake hand and say goodbye/run out of time

It is important of course not to follow a strict 'formula', but you do need a basic scheme or you won't have any structure at all. This is one of the main conflicts in the CSA—structure vs. formulaic consulting. I feel this schema is a good compromise between the two, but feel free to tweak it and of course remember that, depending on the patient's agenda, it is absolutely fine to do things out of order, or even add new bits and leave bits out where you need to. This is above all not a strict formula—it is simply a guide to help you structure your consultations for the CSA exam.

So to summarise so far: we have learnt that the key to passing the CSA is to have a **structure that is neither so structured that it is formulaic, nor so loose that there is no structure and that it is therefore disordered.** We have also learnt that the key skill being tested is the **ability to discover what the patient wants from the consultation, ascertain what you want to do with the patient** (having made some sort of diagnosis or a diagnosis of 'uncertainty') and then use the glue of communication skills to bind these together into a **reasonable plan, that the patient is happy with, and that you feel is safe.**

It is time to look at this communication skill 'glue'.

Communication Skills

Introduction:

In this chapter, the main chapter of the book, I am going to give you a whole lot of ideas to consider incorporating into your consultations. No-one will use all of them in one consultation; that would be impossible. Instead this is a just a brief overview of many techniques that people use to make parts of the consultation go more smoothly. You will perhaps already know many of them and may use them in your consultations. This is great; why not try some of the ones you don't regularly use? You may find that some 'just don't work' for you, that is fine as well, everyone consults differently.

In his book, 'The Inner Consultation', Neighbour suggests that a good way to learn a new skill is to write it down on a post-it note, shuffle it up with other skills you are trying to learn, and then, before the patient walks in, pull one out.[3] Try to use that skill in this consultation. This technique is an option. Another possibility is to write down a new consultation skill that you are trying to improve onto a card and put it just under your surgery PC screen, try using it in every consultation that morning. By the end of the morning it may have finally found its way into your cerebellum and be a 'learnt behaviour', from now on it is in your 'toolbox' of consultation skills, ready to be got out and used whenever you need it. You can now start on another skill. If you start this early enough and practice in your small groups, by the time you sit the exam you should have quite a full toolbox—full of tools that you understand and can apply subconsciously at the right time. Tools that will not only impress the examiners and score you plenty of CSA points, but tools that will also make your consultations better for years to come.

Openings:

'Please state the nature of the medical emergency.'

The Doctor - Star Trek Voyager.

How do you normally start your consultations?

Most people find that they start almost every consultation the same way. Is the way you start your consultations helpful? Why do you start them this way?

The reason this matters in the CSA is twofold: rapport and time. You need to develop a good rapport to help the case unfold nicely, and you also need to make every question count, you only have ten minutes.

In real life we talk of the 'golden minute': the time at the start of the consultation where, if you have opened it well, the patient is likely to tell you a huge amount of useful information. Your opening statement needs to encourage the patient to do this.

My usual opening statement always was:

'Hi, I'm Dan, good to meet you. How can I help you today?'

But I'm not sure this is the best opening you can have; it has a major drawback. It interrupts the patient. Real patients, sitting in the waiting room, spend a fair bit of time thinking of what they will say first when they walk in to the room. They will rehearse it, often over and over, trying to work out how they are going to explain to you what is bothering them. In the same way, the actor in the exam has a statement prepared that he may start the case with. So if you start the consultation by asking a question, you run the risk of just getting an answer to that question, essentially you run the risk of jeopardising 'the golden minute'.

People have lots of ways round this. My trainer suggested to me that I try complete silence, just wait for them to start. But people often just seemed to... not start! So I ended up sitting awkwardly until I eventually asked: 'how can I help you today?'

But then I found that if I greeted patients at the door, shook their hand and introduced myself, gestured to their seat, *'please have a seat'*, and sat down, that the patient would often burst into full flow with no need for a further word from me. I'm not sure if I'm imagining it, but I think I get more out of these consultations, and this technique did seem to work for me in the CSA.

Of course there is no absolute right or wrong. I don't think it is *wrong* to ask, 'how can I help you today?' But if you haven't ever tried an alternative then perhaps practice a few other options that are more open and see what the responses are. You may be surprised, and you may find your CSA consultations yielding more useful information in the first, crucial, couple of minutes.

First Impressions:

In terms of non verbal communication it's important to get your own non verbal cues correct. The exam is really quite scary, so you need to go out of your way to pretend it isn't affecting you. Put on an extra big smile. When the bell goes off, say 'come in', in as friendly a voice as you can. Get up from your seat and meet the patient half way. Shake them by the hand if you feel comfortable doing this. I really think handshakes are a great idea (the physical contact gets you easy extra rapport points), but if you really hate handshaking by all means avoid it.

So, you've met the patient half way, got them into a chair, and you have used some sort of opening line (or no opening line). The patient is talking. They tell you a symptom. Try not to interrupt them. Let them speak until they dry up (which may be a much shorter period of time in the CSA than in real life). Feel free to nod, look interested and even make the odd noise to show that you have taken a point on board, but avoid actually saying any words.

When they have finally stopped talking it is time to try to get some more rapport.

Summary:

- Consider your opening statement, how open is it? Could it be more open? Do you need to start the consultation at all? Discuss and find what works for you

- Be friendly, even though the exam is scary, get up and greet the patient

- Do not interrupt the patient's opening statements

Rapport:

'When it comes to reassuring a traumatised nineteen year old, I'm about as expert as a palsy victim doing brain surgery with a pipe wrench.'

Hartigan - Sin City

Rapport is essentially the ability to enter the patient's world enough to understand it.[1]

The best way to achieve good rapport with a patient is to do it genuinely; it is very hard to 'fake'. If you really are genuinely interested in why the patient is here, what they are worried about, and you really want to get to the bottom of it and help them, then this will come across. The main skill, as regards rapport in the CSA, is to try to prevent the unusual circumstances from preventing your natural rapport from coming out. To achieve this you need to try to reduce your stress levels. One option is to try to pretend it is not an exam but instead a locum GP session. But with the added advantage that you will definitely never need to see any of the patients again, get sued by any of them, or write any notes about them! Discuss in your small groups and try to find an idea that you think might work for you.

Mirroring:

In general terms one of the best ways to think about rapport is to observe two people who are in love. Next time you are in a bar or coffee shop try to do some people watching. What do people do when they are talking to someone they want to connect with? The main thing you might notice is something called 'mirroring'. This is when two people, completely subconsciously, do similar things with posture, voice tone and eye movements. They are in synchrony and they show it externally. This is believed to be an evolutionary mechanism we have learnt, and it's controlled not by the cerebral cortex, but by the limbic system;[4] as a result it is usually entirely subconscious. This is great for us. If we can consciously (and subtly) mirror the patient in terms of posture, tone etc, for the first couple of minutes in the consultation, we can make them subconsciously warm to us more. They are more likely to feel that we are someone who they feel comfortable speaking too, someone who really listens. This will get you marks in the CSA, and in real life will make your consultations much more useful and fulfilling. If you make a conscious effort to try this, you will suddenly realise that you begin to do it subconsciously after a few consultations of practicing this skill.

To further emphasise the importance of mirroring. Think about a consultation, perhaps observing a consultant in clinic when you were a junior doctor, where the consultant spent the whole time looking through the patient's notes. Even if they welcomed them verbally when they came into the room the patient probably feel quite cold towards them, and the consultation probably took longer and was less satisfactory to all parties as a result. It was made dysfunctional through poor body language.

If you show poor body language to the patient, for instance: folding your arms, not looking at them when speaking to them, flicking through the notes on the ipad etc, they are likely to feel colder towards you. Interestingly, if asked, they probably won't know exactly why they don't take to you, it's subconscious. Your posture has made them feel that here is someone who is more interested in their own work than them. This might be completely unreasonable, but since it is subconscious they cannot reason it, they just 'don't take to you'. You don't want a patient actor in the CSA feeling this way about you.

I think it is always worth having quite an open posture when a patient comes into the room, perhaps sat slightly forwards (but not too far) in your chair, arms not folded, palms slightly up if possible. It's important to try to look natural despite this of course, so you don't want to take it too far.

An advanced technique which is quite useful is to take mirroring and use it to subtly change a patient's affect. We could call this technique counter-mirroring. For instance, if a patient comes in and seems shy, or doesn't really want to engage, you can try to use mirroring to help them engage. You might think that being as open and confident as possible is the way to go here, but oddly this can sometimes shut down a patient who feels this way even further. Instead why not try matching their posture subtly, like you would do usually. This might require you to adopt a slightly closed position and perhaps alter your tone of voice, speaking more quietly for instance. You are trying to mimic them a bit, but without making yourself look too shy or withdrawn of course. After a minute or so of doing this whilst consulting, the patient will hopefully have subconsciously noticed that your postures are mirrored. During the consultation you may then be able to slip back into an open posture and find that the patient will subconsciously do the same. The rapport you have created with them has allowed you to move them subconsciously into a more open posture, they mirrored *you!* This likely will have the knock on effect of making the patient less anxious and afraid and more comfortable speaking to you, although again they are not likely to know why. They may have a feeling that you understand them, and are someone they can trust. They may then tell you what it is that is really worrying them.

Jargon:

Another facet to good rapport, throughout the whole consultation, is to avoid the use of jargon. This is really difficult for doctors, because we have been speaking another language for so long that we have probably forgotten that some of what we don't consider 'jargon'—is certainly considered jargon by some patients.

To avoid jargon you need to be attuned to the patient in front of you. It's impossible to make a perfect generalisation about a person, but just listening to their own language can help you establish what type of words you might be able to use. However, don't assume though that a patient who uses simple language, and doesn't seem too 'knowledgeable', doesn't want a detailed explanation of what is going on. Why not ask him how much he wants to know before diving in on a long explanation? That could save you a lot of time, and the patient a lot of confusion.

A good way to avoid jargon is to explain any 'medical word' in other words. For instance 'erythema', in ancient Greek, simply means 'red skin', so why not do the translation for them, and just say 'red skin'. In the heat of the moment it's really hard to remember to do this, particularly if we are stressed; so you need to practice. Ask people in your practice group to watch out for jargon when you use it and point it out to you. That way it will become second nature.

Sometimes there might be a word, such as the name of a condition, 'idiopathic thrombocytopenic pupura', for instance, that you will need to actually say to the patient. Signposting again can be your friend here, explain to them that their condition has a medical name, that it is long, and perhaps could sound scary, explain what the words mean, then let them know the name.

e.g. *'...essentially it is a rash caused by low levels of something called platelets, in the blood. The long name is ...... I can print out some more information about it which you can have a read about later, and I can explain more about it to you here as well, if you like.'*

You might have to go on to explain what platelets are if the patient isn't sure. If in doubt always check.

e.g. *'do you want me to tell you more about that?'* or *'can I just check, what do you already know about platelets?'*

Using and being aware of your Personality:

Feel free when consulting to be yourself. Use your personality to your advantage. Just make sure that you are aware of what your personality is, and how that can affect your consultations with different types of patients.

You might have noticed that certain types of patients seem to just 'click' with you. You consult them well, they seem to enjoy seeing you, and you feel the consultations go very well. You'll have probably also noticed that there are certain groups of patients you find it very hard to connect with. This is probably to do with your personality and your natural style of consulting.

In the CSA you will have a wide range of different patients, some of whom might be from groups you normally find it hard to consult fluidly. These are the groups that you need to work on, try to think of why you find it hard to consult these people.

Often, older people are used to doctors being authoritarian. They may also find that younger people who speak quickly, and may seem almost overly familiar, are difficult to connect with. This is of course a massive generalisation, but many young GPs and registrars I have spoken to have felt that the way we are taught to communicate, and specifically our emphasis on patient centeredness, can often be at odds with what this older patient group wants.

Younger people can often respond well to a doctor who seems 'quirky', someone who clearly has their own interesting life. But sometimes teenagers can sometimes see you as a completely unapproachable figure, even though you may in reality only actually be a few years older than they are. You may be quite frightening to them. Again generalisations, but you have perhaps experienced similar things yourself.

If you find that a particular group of patients presents you with certain challenges, then try to think about why that is. They may well be picking up on an aspect of your personality and finding it is getting in the way of their consultation with you. Perhaps a patient finds that you speak too quickly and don't offer the concrete answers they expect. Or perhaps they see your careful questioning and analysis of their symptoms as signs that you are a boring robot (hopefully you're not!). Try to think of ways of slightly altering your expression of your personality traits in these situations; not changing who you are but simply adjusting to the person in front of you. Stay yourself, but if you feel a patient is finding something you are doing irritating, try to tone it down. The more you look out for aspects like this in the consultation, the more that you will become attuned to noticing when something isn't quite right. This is the first step towards tailoring your consultations individually to the person in front of you—increasing rapport, saving time, and potentially increasing the accuracy of the history you obtain.

Active Listening:

The final point to mention about rapport is that of 'active listening'.

You have probably had your trainer tell you that you need to try to listen more to the patient, and speak less. This is true, but to truly listen in the way your trainer means you need to listen actively.

When the patient is talking, look interested. You can try a practical experiment with a friend to see the importance of this:

Sit down, and for one minute tell the 'patient' about something you are really interested in, a hobby, a sport you play, or an awesome holiday you have been on. Look at what the person does when they are listening; even though they are not speaking they are still probably making certain noises, their expressions change depending on what you are saying. If what you are talking about is *really* interesting they might even ask you a question at the end.

Now, try it again with another subject, but instruct the other person to listen as if you were on TV, i.e. they can't interact with you. It is really very difficult to talk for even a minute under these circumstances, no matter how interesting the subject matter.

The first time I experienced this was the very first time that I was on the radio. I was interested in the subject matter for sure—I had to speak about my debut novel; I was really looking forward to it, but when it came to it, I was basically sitting in a little box. I couldn't see the presenter easily without craning my neck, and listeners at home could not, of course, see me either. I found as I answered questions put to me by the host that because I could not see her face, I found it very hard to talk for long on anything at all. This was because I was getting no feedback. Interestingly, speaking clearly without receiving feedback is, like almost anything, a skill that can be learnt, and having been on the radio many times now I am no longer as nonplussed by this. I still remember that strange first time though.

This is why it is so important to actively listen to patients. Without the little nods, sounds, and occasional open questions they will also dry up and the useful information that you need to get out of them will become much harder to extricate.

As you actively listen to the patient try to pick up on any cues. These can come in many forms. The patient could become uncomfortable when mentioning something, or they may say a particular phrase:

e.g. *'I think I'm going to have to take time off work again.'*

These cues may not be best tackled at the time they are said if the patient has moved on to another subject, or you need to ask something else important first, but try to remember the cue, or even scribble it down if you have to. Then you can use them later. This is the epitome of active listening and the examiners will really like it. It strikes the right balance between structure and not being formulaic, and it shows that you treat the consultation like a conversation—tailored to that person sitting in front of you at that time, not the same old list of questions you ask everyone.

e.g. 'earlier on you mentioned that you thought you might have to take time off work again. Are you worried that this, INSERT SYMPTOM HERE, might be affecting your ability to work?'

The patient may then spill the beans about the fact that he is self employed, has barely any money and needs to work to look after his disabled daughter etc. You may not be able to change any of this, but realising what is worrying him will net you extra rapport and allow you to tackle management later, armed in advance with the knowledge that time off work may be a difficult area to negotiate for instance.

In the CSA, it is important to remember that any verbal cue given to you by a patient is probably very important to the case. Ensure you pick up on them at some point. As mentioned it is absolutely fine to come back to them later if you need to discuss something else first, but don't forget.

Summary:

- Be genuinely interested in the patient

- Actively learn methods to reduce your stress

- Try 'mirroring', and use it to generate rapport and possibly alter patient mood and behaviour

- Avoid jargon, when you have to use jargon: 'signpost'

- Use active listening

ICE and how to 'really' use it:

'I'm not a magician, Spock, just an old country doctor.'

Dr Leonard McCoy - Star Trek the Original Series - 'The Deadly Years'

I remember the first time I was properly introduced to ideas, concerns, expectations. I was an F2 doctor doing my first ever experience in General Practice. My supervisor asked me what I knew about ICE. I really had no idea what she meant at all, so she broke the acronym down, and it began to dawn on me what she meant. It was cheating. I couldn't understand how this could work, surely patients would see through it? Patients come to see us so that we can figure out what is wrong, and tell them what to do to make it better. If we turn round and ask them what they think is wrong and what they think we should do about it, then surely they'll either think we are being sarcastic, or worse, incompetent!

She suggested I try it.

At first I had mixed success, this practice, like my current practice, is in the middle of nowhere in rural Cumbria. The farmers who came to see me would often say: 'you're the doctor', if I asked them what they thought might be going on. Or: 'whatever you think doctor', if I asked them what they were hoping we might do for them.

But I not only found out how to get around these problems, I also discovered that Ideas, Concerns, and Expectations, despite my initial misgivings, is absolutely critical to consulting. Although patients may believe that they are coming to the doctor just to get our opinion on a problem, the same way I might take my car to the garage and go: 'it's not working, please sort it out', they have a lot more investment in themselves than I do in my car. Deep down, they all have anxieties, worries, and ideas. Being English often makes the way they express this dilemma between expressed absolute trust, and suppressed mild distrust, highly dysfunctional; we want to respect doctors, but deep down we have a secret worry that perhaps they don't really know what is going on[5]. This interferes with the consultation, and can often be the reason why in a consultation you can sometimes feel that things just aren't, 'going anywhere.'

Essentially to break this you need to understand that almost every consultation has some element of tension between what you, as the doctor, think is going on (and what you think needs to be done), and what the patient thinks is going on (and what they are thinking you should do).

Most people are completely happy to go along with your plan, after all they did come to you for advice, but they really really want to know that you have considered what they originally thought the problem was, even if you go on to show them that their initial ideas were wrong. ICE, used cleverly, is the way to do this. It is not, 'cheating'. But perversely, patients might feel it *is* if you make it too obvious, and this is probably why we feel a bit uncomfortable using it.

Despite our slight underlying distrust of doctors, we would ideally like them to be mind readers. My wife, who is not medical, still expects that her doctor will be able to magically tell her what is wrong just by examining her. Patients do not often appreciate how important the history is, and in particular the points of a history that can only come out when a patient is open with what they are worrying about. We are expected to be both doctors and magicians, when ICE is the only real trick up our sleeve.

'Softening' ICE:

So, we have established how important it is to use ICE; and how it can make our consultations run more smoothly, whilst also being more patient centred. These are key CSA skills. What we need to do now is explore how to use ICE in a non formulaic way that doesn't result in the patient saying, 'well, you're the doctor, how am I supposed to know what is wrong with me?' You will also I think find that these techniques make you feel a lot more comfortable asking these questions too. Try saying these examples below out loud and see what you think.

One of the best tools to use here, is again, signposting.

Look at the difference between these.

A: *'What do you think might be going on here?'*

B: *'You seem to have been putting up with this for a long time/this seems to have been causing you an awful lot of bother - have you had any thoughts about what might be going on?*

There are lots of ways to do this, so the example above is just that, an example. The phrase before the question could be considered a 'softener'. You are showing some empathy, and you are also letting the question, that you are a bit awkward about, slip out straight after it—it just follows on from something that both you and the patient are comfortable talking about. The patient is far more likely to answer your question in B, than they are in A. They are also more likely to not notice that it is a 'strange' question.

Another example:

A: *'Is there something you are really worried about here?'*

B: *'Sometimes when people have symptoms like this it really concerns them. Often they feel it must be something really serious. Have you been feeling like this?'*

Obviously you need to use common sense here, don't feel you have to ask every patient about concerns. Sometimes the concerns might not be medical either; perhaps they are worried they might lose their job. Try to pick up on any verbal, visual, or note based cues to guide any questions about concerns. In the example above, the patient, who you perhaps think might be worried their tension headache is in fact cancer, may now feel able to mention this underlying worry to you without feeling 'stupid'.

The use of the word, 'concern', in the example above is purposeful. The word, 'worry', actually has quite a few negative connotations in British culture: the patient could construe that you think they are a 'worrier'. Feel free to use the word 'concerns', the patient doesn't know the ICE acronym, there is no problem using the words straight out of the acronym if this is appropriate. Bear in mind what you are trying to achieve—you are not trying to pretend that you are being one hundred percent original to the examiner. This ICE acronym is well known and is useful; you don't have to try disguising that you are using it. Just think about how you ask the questions, keeping them grounded in what the patient has already said where possible. If it's tailored to the patient, in the same way a conversation would be, then it's not formulaic.

Another example:

A: *'What did you think we might do for you today?'*

B: *'When you were walking up to the surgery/booking the appointment today, did you have any thoughts about what we might do to help you/investigate this?*

Again, it takes longer to say B (only a few seconds though), but by grounding it in the patient's life it is less formulaic and is 'softer' for the patient. It doesn't sound so pre-prepared or formulaic.

You could equally well ask about expectations based on what a patient has said.

e.g. *'You mentioned earlier that you were fed up with seeing us so many times about this, and were worried we hadn't got to the bottom of it. I wondered if you had any particular hopes about what we might do today.'*

Here you have done two things: acknowledged the patient's frustration at a perceived lack of progress (gaining rapport), and also potentially accessed their underlying hopes about what they think needs done. This patient could also have some underlying concerns which you could have asked about instead in exactly the same way. As a general rule, try to base questions on what has been said before and try to pick up on phrases the patient has said and use them to generate new questions. The patient will feel listened to, and if the question is somewhat awkward (like these ICE questions) they are far more likely to answer and not feel the question was especially unusual.

An important point to make, that covers the whole of this section is that whatever the patient says in response to ICE do not challenge it at this stage[3]. It is really important to allow the patient to express their ICE to you without being shot down. The management part of the consultation is where you need to try to splice their ICE and your ICE together.

A Last Resort:

So the point of ICE is to try to find out why the patient has come, but what if it doesn't work? I suspect that you, just like myself, have had consultations where, despite trying your best, you still feel you have not got to the bottom of things. This can happen in the CSA, either because you have missed something important, or because part of the case is to test how you deal with a patient with a hidden agenda. If there is a hidden agenda, your best chance of revealing it lies in looking for and picking up on cues and doing ICE thoughtfully as above whilst establishing a good rapport. But if all else fails, and you still feel you have 'missed the point' then why not share this with the patient?

e.g. *'I'm really sorry, but we have been talking for a couple of minutes now, and I'm still not really sure how best I can help you. I feel perhaps I have missed the point a little. Is there something particularly bothering you?'*

It would be scary to deliver a line such as this in the CSA, but sometimes we need to share our uncertainty with patients in order to move forwards.

Summary:

- Do not be afraid to openly use ICE in the exam

- ICE is the key to determining the patient's side to the dilemma of the consultation

- Try to 'soften' the questions with a warm up phrase to make them less awkward

- Try to base your questions on phrases said earlier by the patient, picking up on cues

- Do not challenge any unusual, ideas, concerns or expectations yet. Save that for the management discussion later

How to use Summarising to your Advantage:

'Things are as they are. Looking out into the universe at night, we make no comparisons between right and wrong stars, nor between well and badly arranged constellations.'

Alan Watts

So, you have obtained a history, perhaps you are going to do an examination. But first you need to ensure you haven't missed anything important. This is especially important in the CSA. Although in real life it would be massively annoying to find that half way through the consultation you have completely missed the point, if you do this in the CSA it is even worse—you will probably fail the case. A good way to avoid this is to look for cues in the patient. In the CSA you can also watch for the actor stumbling as they try to think of answers to questions they have never been asked before, a sure way of knowing you have moved off track. But to be on the safe side, before you leave history taking for good try to make a brief summary back to the patient; this will hopefully help clear up any misunderstandings.

A good summary also has the benefit of showing the patient that you have been listening, which will generate more rapport. Finally, it gives you a chance to gather your thoughts and think about the most difficult part of the consultation, the management section.

Try not to make the summary long, just 30 seconds or so. Try to use the patient's language if possible, this again shows that you have been listening.[1]

Observe the patient closely as you summarise and if they seem surprised by something you have said, check it further with them. You may have missed something, and now is pretty much the last chance to catch it. Then, once you have finished, ask whether you have got it right. Hopefully you will have done, in which case your confidence levels will rise nicely going into the last part of the consultation. If not, the patient may well fill in an important gap for you.

Using a Summary to Signpost your Management:

One advanced trick that could help you in tricky circumstances is using the summary as a way of 'setting up' the management. For instance, I once consulted a lady who had come to see me for blood results. They had seen a colleague a week or two ago as they were tired all the time. I was worried this was going to be a really difficult consultation, because the results were normal. The lady had quite a high powered job and was young, I imagined that she probably would be concerned that we hadn't got to the bottom of the problem and would want 'more tests'. I told her the results, took a bit of a history to ensure that nothing obvious was missed (depression, red flags etc) and then summarised as follows:

'Ok, so just to make sure I've not missed anything. Over the last few months you have noticed that you have been getting increasingly tired. You noticed this all starting around the same time as you went back to work full time, six months after little Alfie was born. You have noticed that you are tired at work, but also at home, and you are worried that work will notice as you have only just gone back. At home your husband works long hours, and you spend most of your time looking after your six month old baby Alfie. You are finding that you have little time to relax, almost no time to yourself, and you have found that sleep is hard to come by as you are woken at least three times every night by Alfie. Was there anything else I missed?'

The lady looked at me, and said.

'When you put it like that... well... that's normal to feel tired like that, isn't it?'

I was able to commiserate with her about how having small children is nice and rewarding, but also rather hard work. She left, happy to see how things went, share with her husband about how hard she was finding life, and come back if things were getting worse.

Think about how you could use a summary to lead a patient to a truth that they are not yet aware of. It can be a very gentle way of altering an incorrect health belief. In cognitive behavioural therapy we would call this 'guided discovery'.

Summary:

- Summarise after your history, it helps you gather thoughts, and makes sure you haven't missed anything

- Check understanding afterwards, and use any queries to clear up the history before moving on

- Consider the use of a 'therapeutic summary', to put a problem into a new perspective for a patient

The Meeting of Two Experts:

'Whatever comes out of these gates, we've got a better chance of survival if we work together. Do you understand? If we stay together, we survive.'

Maximus - Gladiator

In the 1980's, Tuckett wrote a book which described how the consultation could be seen as a 'meeting between two experts'.[6] Visualising the consultation in this way can particularly help when trying to run a doctor led, patient centred consultation. The reason I think the analogy is useful is that it does not insist that the consultation is 'equal'. Ultimately the patient has come to see you for your advice: this is not an equal relationship. But, at the same time their point of view is important—without it you will fail to meet their expectations, which will damage compliance and their likelihood of consulting you again in the future, but on top of that you may miss a crucial part of the history and may get the diagnosis utterly wrong.

Even though you are the medical expert and you must **lead** the consultation, the consultation is about the patient, who should be the **centre** of it. As the centre of the consultation, his responsibility is to also act as an expert, on his own symptoms.

It's important to get these concepts of leading and 'centredness', the right way round. All too often we try to make a consultation so patient centred that we might as well not be there. The patient is relying on us to interpret their symptoms and signs correctly, use our knowledge to determine what plans might be safe, and then provide a plan that is suitable to the patient, taking into account their own special circumstances. We cannot do this if the patient is also leading the consultation. Examples of being too patient led might include:

- Feeling that you need to offer a course of management which would not be suitable for the illness you have diagnosed.
- Taking on too many problems in one consultation rather than setting a reasonable agenda with the patient.
- Not explaining the pros and cons of options enough for the patient to make an informed choice, just listing options and letting them choose.
- Being pressurised into a course of action by the patient, against your better judgment.

As long as you stay in control of the consultation, it is good to allow the patient to help it flow. Work at their pace, and use your active listening skills to feel your way through. Determine all the information you need from your patient 'expert'. Then use your own expertise to turn it into a possible, and safe, shared plan.

Summary:

- The patient is an expert in their symptoms

- You are an expert in medicine

- Stay patient centred but doctor led

- Don't feel you have to do anything a patient asks you too, but always be considerate and explain yourself

Making a Plan Truly Shared:

'All compromise is based on give and take, but there can be no give and take on fundamentals. Any compromise on mere fundamentals is a surrender. For it is all give and no take.'

Mahatma Ghandi

So, you have determined what the patient wants from you. You know about their background, and you have some good ideas about what they think is going on, and what their worries are.

You have also taken a great history, excluded serious red flags, and double checked a couple of important points in their medical history. You may have even examined them. Six minutes are up, and you are ready to move on. This is the moment where you wrap the case up and send the patient away with a credible plan that, ideally, they are happy with.

If what they think is going on, and what you think is going on are the same then you are in luck! This may sometimes actually be the case in real life, but in the CSA it is more than likely that there will be some difficulties here below the surface. It is likely that what the patient wants, or is expecting, will be in some way mismatched with your findings and plan. If it were not this way, then there would be no test.

Explanations:

The first step to being able to develop a shared management plan is to explain to the patient what you think is going on. This requires significant practice. You need to be able to explain complex concepts quickly and in simple language. As mentioned earlier you need to handle jargon carefully.

To practice explanation you ideally need small groups. Use a set of case cards (the RCGP produce their own set) and take it in turns to explain a concept to one of your colleagues. Set yourself an absolute maximum of one minute to do this, ideally thirty seconds. You'll be surprised at how difficult it can be to explain simple concepts to a lay person within tight time constraints. In the exam when you are being watched by two people you will find it even harder. Therefore you need to be able to explain common concepts in your sleep. Practice this skill.

Once you have got really good at explaining conditions concisely to patients, then you can move up a level and can use your explanation to potentially set up your agenda as well:

e.g. '.....tension headache is not a 'serious' condition, but that doesn't mean it can't have a serious effect on your life. However, it is not going to cause severe harm to you, and is not related to cancer.....'

Sometimes if you feel there is going to be real tension though between what the patient wants, and what you want, you need to deal with it even earlier than this. This is to avoid resentment building and ruining the consultation. Neurolinguistic programming can help here.

Using NLP:

The first step is to try to put yourself in the patient's position. Neurolinguistic programming people would call this the '2nd position'. You need to imagine that you are the patient, living their life, with their symptoms, worries, and expectations. Trying to experience this from their perspective will help you see what potential problems they might have with your plan.

Neurolinguistic programming would now suggest you need to adopt a position known as 'meta'. By combining the two, you may be able to see where conflict may lie before it happens. The next step is to address it as neatly as possible so as to avoid dysfunction in the consultation.

Dealing with conflict before it happens:

This is the most important part of this whole chapter. If you feel that a patient isn't going to like your plan, the absolute worst thing you can do is act like a salesman on the phone. They are taught to just keep talking, don't let the target speak and eventually they will get a sale. You might get the patient to superficially agree by doing this (you may also get an angry patient!) but you are highly unlikely to get concordance with your plan (or any marks!).

If you feel a patient isn't going to like your plan you need to be honest. Tell them.

Signposting, yet again.

e.g. *'You mentioned earlier how hard it might be to take time off work, I can see how being self employed would make this really difficult. But I think we should maybe talk about this option more.'*

Or

e.g. *'I know you wanted to be referred immediately to see a neurologist about this headache, and I can see that you want this because you are very concerned this is something serious, in particular cancer. However, I think we need to consider other possibilities too. I*

68

would like to talk about this more so that we can try to find a plan together.'

Or

e.g. *'this can be difficult can't it? You were probably expecting your blood results to show a reason for feeling so tired. It can be a funny mixture of emotions when everything comes back normal, part of you may well be relieved, but a part of you wonders: 'what is going on then?''*

Then 'feel' your way through from there. This is a situation where you should allow the patient to lead a little. Don't feel pressured to act in an unsafe way, or misuse resources, but be respectful of the patient's position and be happy to offer compromise as long as it is a reasonable and safe compromise.

Options and compromise:

Once you have shown good active listening, and shown the patient that you appreciate why the plans you are about to give them could be difficult for them, you can then start to lay the plans out slowly. This is where you need to be most patient centred. Try to be thick skinned, the patient may not want to do exactly what you would normally do in this situation. Try to see it from their point of view, their preferred plan may be just as safe as the plan you would usually recommend first line.

If possible give the patient options. The key here is to explain why there are options. Feel free to offer options which are perhaps not your number one choice of treatment but which might suit the patient, but don't offer options you would not be happy to go along with. If the option the patient is hoping for is one which you would not be happy to go along with you need to get this out of the way first, don't avoid having the conversation just because it might be difficult; it's probably where the marks are for this case.

As you lay out options, try to briefly explain the pros and cons of each. You do not have time to go into detail at the moment though; just lay out a few brief pros and cons. Once you have given options, ask the patient their thoughts. They will probably ask for more detail about one or two of the options.

Remember if referring, that it is probably best to offer referral options that are available to you locally. That way you won't get caught up trying to 'imagine' you are working in central London where the exam is set. In rural Cumbria for instance we can directly request knee MRI, which raised a surprised glance from one of my colleague's examiner! However it turns out that in London, if someone has palpitations they get referred to a 'palpitations clinic' rather than seeing my practice nurse to get fitted with our ancient portable ECG machine, which I then have to try to interpret the results of!

In some circumstances the patient may not need to make a decision right now. This is particularly likely if a decision is being made about non emergency referral. Allow the patient time to talk their thoughts through with you, explain as much as you can, and offer a leaflet with further information. Let them come back and further discuss the plan or give you a call in a few days.

Once you have given options that you are happy with, discussed the pros and cons of each, and tried to help the patient match some of the options with their own agenda, you have created a fully shared management plan. Most of the cases in the CSA will end like this; the patient will appear happy with the plan and then leave. It doesn't necessarily mean that the plan is correct though. Even though the exam is not predominately testing knowledge, make sure your knowledge is up to scratch—it should be at this point anyway, you are about to be a real GP.

Dealing with conflict:

Inevitably there will be cases in the CSA where the patient is not going to see your side of things. They might be adamant about a certain course of treatment for instance, or they might be demanding a referral. On the other hand, they might not be taking a serious diagnosis seriously enough, e.g. refusing to go to hospital when there is a suspected heart attack.

In these situations you need to remain calm, and you need to remember that you cannot make the patient do what you want. You need to remain polite. It is important though to make your ırly. The methods to avoid conflict shown earlier are ıys of showing a patient why their plan may not be the y now need to be more direct. Explain politely, but clearly, why you cannot refer the patient; offer a compromise if one is available, but do not feel compelled to follow a course of action that is poor use of resources or is dangerous.

Remember that part of that particular case's marking will relate to how you deal with the dilemma. Do not feel pressurised to act in a way different to how you would act in real life. However, where possible show compromise; try to see things from the patient's perspective and keep reflecting to the patient that you are doing this. If reasonable agreement is difficult try to get to some sort of 'middle ground' with the patient that would be acceptable, but not necessarily preferable, to both of you.

Patient refusing life saving treatment:

If a patient is refusing important treatment, explain why it is so important that they consider accepting the treatment, ensure any barriers to the treatment have been explored and then if they remain non compliant see if you need to check capacity.

To have capacity a patient must be able to[8]:

- understand the information relevant to the decision
- retain that information
- use or weigh that information as part of the process of making the decision

- communicate their decision (whether by talking, using sign language or any other means)

You must assume a patient has capacity unless you have evidence to the contrary. If you suspect the patient may not have capacity, i.e. you think they are suffering from a form of mental impairment, e.g. delirium from sepsis, then test them against the points above.

An example of how to do this is:

D: *OK. Mr Smith, I have explained that this severe pain in your tummy could well be due to an infection in your abdomen. My examination of your tummy has suggested that this is likely and that the best treatment for this is to go to hospital and see a surgeon. I understand that you do not want to attend hospital. Can I just check, what do you think the worst that could happen is if you don't attend hospital?*

P: *I'm not sure doctor. I guess the pain wouldn't get better?*

D: *That may be the case, but the worst that could happen, I'm sorry to say, is that you could die if this infection is not treated early. Hopefully this wouldn't happen of course, but there is a risk.*

P: *Oh, I don't like the sound of that doc!*

D: *Can I ask you again then, what is your understanding now of the worst thing that could happen if you don't attend hospital?*

P: *Well, I could die!*

D: *That is right. Is your mind still made up? You are free to choose to not go in if you want to, but is there anything we could discuss that might change your mind?*

In the example above, the patient seems to have capacity to make this decision. It is important to remember that as long as a patient has capacity to make a particular decision, then they are free to make a very unwise decision should they so wish.

Summary:

- Start by discussing any major discrepancies between agendas

- Give a good, concise and jargon free explanation of the diagnosis

- To avoid conflict, try to anticipate it and deal with it before the patient brings it up

- Try to imagine how the patient would feel about the different options

- Explain the pros and cons of options, and give the patient any help they need in making a decision

- Do not offer options that you feel are not safe or suitable

- Be honest with the patient

- Where there is intractable conflict, try to reach middle ground

- Accept that patients with capacity may make unwise decisions to refuse treatment

Admitting that you don't know what is going on:

'As far as the laws of mathematics refer to reality, they are not certain; and as far as they are certain, they do not refer to reality.'

Albert Einstein

There are patients in the CSA whose aim is to specifically test how you deal with uncertainty.

If you think about your everyday practice you see at least one person a session, and probably more, to whom you cannot give a firm diagnosis. This is because in general practice we see patients much earlier than they are usually seen in secondary care. We see illness before it has had a chance to fully develop, or disappear.

This creates two problems:

- We run the risk of worrying about and investigating illness which isn't there – the patient comes back in a few days or weeks and is completely better. We have maybe scared ourselves and the patient, and wasted resources.

- We run the risk of missing something serious until it has developed further than we would have liked. Perhaps we had falsely reassured the patient?

The examiners want to see how you deal with this situation. The most important aspect to this dilemma is again communication. Despite what you might expect, most patients really don't mind you admitting that you cannot tell them exactly what is going on. What they usually want to know is that you don't think it is serious, that you have a plan to follow things up, and that you have understood their concerns.

Use their concerns as part of the explanation to help show the patient that you have taken their point of view on board.

e.g. *'So, I know that you have been really worried about this feeling of 'dizziness' that you describe, and I know that you were really worried about having a fall as a result. I can see how being quite elderly and living alone must be rather worrying for you with these symptoms. The good news is that I haven't managed to find anything wrong yet.*

The symptoms you are describing can come from several parts of your body, and nothing immediately shows itself to be abnormal. Whilst this is a good thing in a way, it can sometimes be a bit scary for a person when their doctor can't give them an answer straight away. Be assured though it is a common situation for us! I find it reassuring that I've found nothing wrong today, but your symptoms are still there, so perhaps we can start by looking at how your symptoms affect you, and what we can do to help there? Perhaps after that we could see how things have developed over the next couple of weeks, to make sure we haven't missed anything?

Go slowly with any sort of explanation like this. Pause, and allow the patient an opportunity to show how their 'active listening' is going. If they seem alarmed, or surprised, give them a chance to speak. Often they will be quite happy with your explanation, and be pleased that you were honest with them, rather than 'blagging'.

Share the difficulty of the situation with the patient, but show them that you have it in hand. Try to deal with the impact of symptoms in the short term, and most importantly give an extra good safety net in these situations. Depending on the presentation you may also want to do some basic investigations, e.g. bloods, but don't feel you have to; only request a test if you have some idea what you are expecting to rule in or rule out.

Summary:

- Feel comfortable with your own limitations

- Feel comfortable with the concept of uncertainty and appreciate why we experience it a lot as GPs

- Practice discussing it with each other in practice cases

- Share the experience with the patient

- Make it clear that you have a safe plan

- Make it clear that you are not dismissing their concerns just because you don't have a name for their condition at the moment

What is really a 'safety net'?

'Come back in two weeks if things aren't settling down, or sooner if it's getting worse.'

Yourself

How often have you heard these words? Coming out of your mouth?

Safety netting can be one of the hardest parts of the consultation, but we often just use a quick throwaway line with little meaning. The reason it is so hard is because it is here where you run the risk of losing the patient's faith in you. You can feel very vulnerable as you suggest the possibility that in fact, despite your best efforts, you might be completely mistaken and things could go hideously wrong!

I think the reason that we often use the throwaway line above is because of some vain hope that it will 'cover us' in the event that the worst happens, and the patient or their family tries to sue us. However, I don't believe that a vague line, like the one at the start of this section will necessarily be strong enough to save you in court. Sometimes I wonder if we say it to try to make ourselves feel better in the face of uncertainty.

Safety netting, essentially, is where we have to come face to face with our own inability to foretell the future. The patient knows we can't do this, but somehow the expectation, from both parties, is that we somehow can predict what will happen with almost one hundred percent accuracy.[9]

In order to safety net better, the first thing we need to do is to come to terms with our own fallibility and own inability to predict the future perfectly. No matter how hard you try and how careful you are, you will make at least one major, and possibly catastrophic, mistake in your time as a GP. You will also be involved in many less major incidents where your plan, no matter how good it was, didn't work. Don't have unrealistic expectations of yourself.

So let your safety nets reflect the truth of the situation; share the knowledge of uncertainty with the patient. Honesty will help promote trust.

e.g. *'these infections usually clear up in around about a week with antibiotics, and it doesn't look bad enough yet for you to need drip antibiotics. I expect that over the next few days the redness will go down and you will feel better. But, there is a small possibility that you might find you start to get a very high fever, feel more unwell, or the redness might even start to spread, or not have gone after a week. If any of that happens please let me know as soon as you can and we may need to rethink the plan. How does that sound?'*

Yes. That took much, much, longer than the first sentence. But the patient in this example knows many things that the throwaway one liner safety net does not give:

- The likely course of the illness
- What the treatment could be if things got worse
- How to know if it's getting worse and what to do
- That you have contemplated what could happen if your initial thoughts were wrong, or if the treatment is ineffective

Not only will they be better educated to deal with their cellulitis, but they will also have an enhanced opinion of you, as their doctor. You will seem more knowledgeable, but yet humble, for you can accept the possibility that you might be wrong. The examiners will likely love it as well.

It's important to mention that the way you deliver this is important. You do not want to come across as indecisive. You need to appear confident in your plan, yet able to accept that things don't always go the way you expect them to. You need to appear confident in taking responsibility for the uncertainty; having developed good rapport during the rest of the consultation really helps here.

Summary:

- Consider spending longer than you currently do safety netting

- Use a safety net to educate the patient

- Be honest about risk and uncertainty

- Specify what the patient should do if things are not playing out as expected

- Use the safety net to empower the patient

Running out of time:

'Time is an illusion. Lunchtime doubly so.'

Ford Prefect - The Hitchhiker's Guide to the Galaxy

There is a clock in the exam room which counts up from zero to ten. Ideally you want to be spending around six minutes on the history and examination, leaving you four to do an explanation, management plan, and safety netting.

As medics though we naturally like doing history taking, and as humans we like to avoid conflict. Subconsciously therefore we don't really want to finish doing the history and move on to the difficult talky bit. You will also find that some of the CSA cases have significantly complex histories or ambiguous presentations. All of this combined can result in you easily overrunning.

Obviously, practicing is the key here. The more you can subconsciously be aware of how long six minutes is, the more your brain will know you need to move on. Practicing in a small group is ideal because it helps you prepare for the exam specifically; I will discuss more about this later in part three of the book. But of course your normal day to day consulting will be extremely useful in practicing time management. Make sure that you are consulting to at least fifteen minute intervals before the exam (ideally ten). In reality the ten minutes you get in the exam is a slight luxury compared to real life consulting (the ten minutes you have per patient in a real surgery has to include waiting for their notes to load, looking at their notes, going and getting them, and then writing up when you have finished).

But despite the best preparation it is extremely easy to run late in this exam, just like in real life. So we need to consider what to do if you look at the clock and see that it says nine minutes, but you have only just finished examining the patient.

Be aware of where the points are in the exam; remember the three domains: Data gathering, management, communication. Don't panic and throw away communication. You have already done data gathering. You are going to lose some management marks by trying to cram all of it into one minute, but you can still get lots if you are careful.

Feel free to make it clear that the consultation needs to move on.

e.g. *'right, we need to move on and have a discussion about how best to help you.'*

Make the explanation as short as possible, a few sentences only. Offer an opportunity for more information in leaflet form perhaps, this will not get you many marks but it's better than none. If there is a 'dilemma' in the case, i.e. a mismatch between your agenda and theirs, try to get into it as soon as possible. Even if you end the case whilst still discussing it, you will not lose points for failing to grasp the dilemma in the consultation.

One final trick is to try to put some safety netting into the explanation, this way you may still get marks for some of it, even though you will not finish the case.

e.g. '......usually tonsillitis improves on its own, but occasionally it does need antibiotics. Sometimes you can get a really severe abscess develop, although this is rare. This could make swallowing impossible, so if you find that it is hard to breath, or you can't swallow fluid, then I suggest you let me know as soon as possible. There are a few options about what we can do to help you, perhaps we could discuss them?...

Summary:

- Practice so that you are less likely to run out of time unawares

- Do not get flustered and potentially lose marks already gained

- Work on getting as many marks as you can in the time you have left

- Try to get straight to the main dilemma of the case if you have not already dealt with it

Special Situations:

This final section of the communication skills chapter is concerned with the special situations that can arise in the CSA. These are consultations that traditionally candidates struggle with. You will not necessarily get all of these, but it is highly likely that you will get one or two. The skills for these are, of course, extremely relevant to everyday practice as well as for the CSA.

Complaint:

'Listen, I am not your enemy, and I can get you home. But first you need to put down that weapon and trust me.'

Jean Luc Picard - Star Trek First Contact

The moment the angry patient walks in and sits down, slamming her bag down on the floor in front of you, your heart sinks. Your heart rate starts to rise, you feel angry yourself; you feel a little afraid. She starts to raise her voice at you. You feel your voice start to rise too. She becomes angrier; you wonder how you are ever going to get out of this situation.

At some point in our lives as doctors we have all dealt with angry patients or their relatives. Often in a hospital situation we were actually instructed to pass them on to a senior member of the team, but now it is our responsibility alone to deal with them. This station in the CSA could be an absolute gift for you as long as you approach it the right way, it is unlikely the medicine will be complicated in this case as it is mainly going to be about testing communication skills. If you know how to deal with it, you can score highly here.

The key to this station is to avoid the description in the first paragraph. Remember 'mirroring' earlier? This is reverse mirroring, or 'transference'. The patient is angry, and a little scared about how you are going to react - so these emotions are passed to you subconsciously. It's human nature to show these emotions, and unfortunately the patient will not realise what they have subconsciously done to you, and will assume that you are uncaring and angry with them. What you need to do is to remember the concept of 'transference'—your emotional response is predominantly a reflection of how upset the person in front of you is. Try to concentrate on remaining calm.

Actively listen to the patient as they tell you what has gone wrong. Let them vent their anger. When they stop, acknowledge their anger.

e.g. *I see that you are really upset/angry about this.*

Then feel free, if it is appropriate, to offer an apology. Do not feel you have to completely and unreservedly apologise if there has been a misunderstanding, or if the patient is being unreasonable, but at least offer some form of apology before trying to explain the situation to them more clearly.

e.g. *'I'm really sorry that you found out about this medication change through the post. I appreciate that you are very angry about this, and wanted to have it explained to you face to face. You feel that this new drug you have been switched to might be a 'poor alternative' to your old medication. Even though I see you are really disappointed with what we have done, I wonder if we could talk about this more, because once I've explained the reason behind the change you might feel happier about it, is that something we can do now?*

This patient is angry about a switch to a generic blood pressure treatment. It is pretty standard to do this, and a lot of patients wouldn't mind. It is reasonable to apologise that the way you let her know made her upset, but in this situation don't feel you need to apologise about the principle, as it is reasonable. However you need to be gentle, as you need to keep the patient onside.

Of course if a serious error has been made, or something has gone badly wrong, feel free to offer a fuller apology to the patient.

e.g. *I'm really sorry this has happened, we haven't got this right at all, and I'm really glad you brought it to my attention right away. I know you are very angry about it, but do you think you would be able to help me by talking with me now about how we could put this right, so that it doesn't happen again?*

This is a full apology, but it also gives the patient a chance to move the consultation on. You are taking responsibility, and that is the key to this type of station. You are also thanking the patient for bringing the problem to you. This will hopefully increase rapport as you are acknowledging that coming and complaining to your doctor is difficult. Be careful not to be 'pass judgement' on your colleagues though if the complaint is about someone else.

Once the patient has calmed down, try to take even more responsibility. Ask the patient what they want done. They may want to make a formal complaint; to do this they will likely need to write to, or make an appointment with, the practice manager. You could offer to help make arrangements for this. It is likely though that they will not want to do this in the CSA as this way there is more scope to discuss the complaint, and this is what the examiners want to see. If the patient just wants to make sure that it can't happen again then you'll need to make a plan with them that both of you are happy with.

Practice meetings are a useful tool here. You could offer to raise the issue at the next meeting and feed back the results of the meeting to the patient. I wouldn't offer the opportunity for the patient to attend that meeting, as in most practices this would not be allowed. However you could arrange a special meeting for the patient with other people involved in the complaint, perhaps offering to discuss the issue with the other people involved first (very useful if the complaint is about one of your colleagues). The patient may have come to you as they don't have the confidence to approach the person the complaint is about, in which case you could again offer to be an intermediary to arrange a meeting between the two, which perhaps you and the practice manager could be at.

It is worth discussing this with your practice manager and making sure you know the local complaints procedure. Also make sure you practice a few different complaint type scenarios in your small group, including if possible a professional type one, where perhaps a nurse from the practice comes to see you to complain about one of the other doctors. The more prepared you are for different eventualities the less thrown you will be. The more composed you are, the more positive 'counter transference' you will exude at the patient and they will subconsciously pick up on your calmness, willingness to listen, and eagerness to put things right.

Summary:

- Remember transference; concentrate on staying calm

- Actively listen

- Offer an apology

- Take responsibility

- Ask the patient what they are hoping you will do

- Know your local procedure for formal complaints

- Practice these cases relentlessly in your group

Breaking Bad News:

Dr. H: *You have twenty-four hours to live.*
Homer: *Twenty-four hours!*
Dr. H: *Well, twenty-two. I'm sorry I kept you waiting so long.*
The Simpsons - One Fish, Two Fish, Blowfish, Blue Fish

This is another case that people often dread. However, it could also be seen as a gift. Essentially it is another case where you don't have to worry about knowing enough medicine or getting the diagnosis 'right'. It's about listening, reflecting, and use of language.

A big worry people have about these cases is where to drop the bombshell. You'll usually have a report from the hospital or a result from a chest X ray etc, which is suspicious for cancer. So you'll know something awful, but the patient won't. My feeling is that it's generally best not to keep them waiting. You might need to ask a few questions, mainly focused on how things have changed since they saw the doctor who requested the test. But put them out of their misery early—don't slavishly follow the standard consultation template and do a six minute history and examination. This case is given to you to test how you deal with an upset patient who you have just given awful news to. Don't avoid the crux of the case.

It is first of all really important to gauge what the patient is expecting. This may well be cued by the patient.

e.g. *'I've been worrying about this all week doc.'* Or: *'it's probably nothing, the locum doc was just being overcautious I reckon.'*

Clearly you cannot be one hundred percent sure of what the patient is really thinking by just hearing these lines; you need to hear the tone of their voice, watch how they sit, see if they look anxious etc. The second line for instance could be false bravado in the face of serious underlying worry about a fatal diagnosis.

If in doubt you could always ask the patient.

e.g. *'I wonder if you could tell me what it was you were thinking the test might show up when you went to have it?'*

It's a bit blunt, and you might get a *'why, is it bad news?'* as an answer, but it's better than just blundering in without any idea of the patient's beliefs.

It's always best to give some sort of warning shot. This may gently start to give some confirmation to their fears:

e.g. *'you mentioned earlier you were worried that this chest X ray could show up something serious, well, unfortunately there are some changes on this X ray that could potentially be worrying.'*

But if the patient doesn't expect at all you may want to be a little softer:

e.g. *'I've got the results here now, I'm afraid it's not great news.'*

Let them take in your warning shot. They will respond to it, and you then need to follow their lead. Feel free to use the cancer word.

e.g. *'really? How serious?'*

Doctor: *'well it's too early to say one hundred percent, but there are some changes on the X ray that we often see in cancer.'*

The key is in the delivery; try to be as calm as you can. Don't be overly emotional, or be so long-winded that the patient gets exasperated or doesn't understand you. Use short sentences in plain English and listen to their responses. Let the patient lead you from here.

Once the blow has set in, ask if they want any more information at the moment. If they want, let them know more about what you have found, what you can do about it at the moment and what further investigations might be needed. Share the fact that it may be too early to make a definitive diagnosis and show that you understand that this can be both scary and frustrating.

You will want to discuss support. Make sure the patient has someone else they can speak to about this and really encourage them to share what is going on with a close friend or family member, they will need the support. You could even offer to call a friend or family member for them if you want; possibly offering to ask them to come and collect them from the surgery later if the patient is very distressed.

Once you have answered any questions they have, it's important to summarise as usual and check the patients understanding. It's common for patients in this situation to not take much in due to the shock. It's important they leave knowing several key things: what the result is, what is the next step (e.g. referral), the answer to any serious questions they had, and when their next follow up is. It is common to offer a follow up within a week with yourself, usually along with a friend or family member if the patient wants. This way any other questions can be answered. Offer written information to go away with too, if the patient wants.

I also often suggest that the patient phones over the next few days if they need to discuss anything. Make it clear to the patient that they are not alone in this problem and you are available if they need help.

It's important not to make promises that you can't keep, be honest about any prognosis and don't make things up. It is very unlikely that we will be able to tell a patient at this stage exactly what is going on, and what will happen. Don't let the patient pressure you into making promises you can't keep as this will destroy their trust in the future and look bad in the exam.

Summary:

- Keep calm
- Break the news early, don't make the patient wait too long
- Establish expectations if possible first
- Warning shot
- Give the patient time to think and ask questions
- Make it clear how supportive you can be
- Don't make promises you can't keep
- Make the follow up plan clear

- Book a review in a few days

Telephone consultation:

This is probably the most difficult consultation you can have. Thankfully in the CSA it is likely the medical content will be relatively simple as, again, the communication is what will be being tested.

The difficulty is the lack of any visual cues since so much of your skill relies on this.

The key to doing well here is to increase your ability to pick up on verbal cues as well as to be even more active in your listening. You don't want to interrupt the patient, but you might want to use more 'uh uh, OK' etc type noises to make sure the patient knows that you are listening. This will have the effect of keeping the history flowing—a verbal equivalent of a nod.

You also need to be very clear in terms of ruling out red flags. You cannot see the patient, so it can be very easy to miss a very sick patient in this station. Make sure you ask about any relevant red flags, and double check anything the patient says that makes you uneasy.

Feel happy with turning down the option of offering treatment over the phone. It often is appropriate to prescribe over the phone, but if you have any doubts at all ask the patient to come in, or even offer a home visit if they sound too ill to come in. Of course emergency situations may even require the use of an emergency 999 call.

Be especially careful with children. Generally it is recommended that children always have a face to face review if acutely unwell[10]. If the family find this difficult, explain the risks associated with not examining the child and try to find a way around whatever barrier there is to them bringing the child in.

Try to practice various scenarios, either actually over the phone, or simulated by sitting back to back with your colleagues. This way you will learn what works and what doesn't. This is a station where having at least one observer is useful when practicing. The observers should try to pick up on any parts of the consultation that felt awkward, and on any really good use of 'active listening' or the picking up of auditory cues. These can then be fed back to the group for learning opportunities.

Finally, with any telephone consultation be explicit in your safety netting—make sure that the patient knows what you expect to happen and when to come for a face to face review or to call for help.

For 2014 it is now possible for telephone consultations to take a slightly different slant: consulting with a colleague. This is likely to take the form of a district nurse or hospital colleague phoning with a concern about a patient.

The key to this is to actively listen and to take seriously the concerns of the colleague. At the start ensure that you know who you are talking to, where they are, and in what way they are involved in the patient's care. Determine what their concerns are, remembering the golden minute as you would normally. Make sure that you have a very good idea what they are wanting you to do within the first two minutes if possible. This then allows you time to ask relevant questions to determine the best course of action. Above all remember to stay respectful and civil, and whatever you do, do not dismiss the person's concerns. Even if you can't see why they are worried about something, remember that they have seen the patient and you have not. Seek to understand their concerns, reassure them when appropriate and ensure that you arrange appropriate treatment and follow up.

There is more on this in the third party consultations section.

Summary:

- The key to telephone consulting is practice

- Focus on active listening and an auditory cues

- Safety net very carefully

- Exclude red flags

- Children should have a face to face review in acute illness[10]

Home Visit:

This is only difficult for two reasons. Firstly the stress of being whisked off from your consulting room and taken to a room where a patient is lying on a bed, and secondly because there is likely to be a complex dilemma.

These stations are home visits for a reason. The patient is likely to be either acutely unwell (in which case the dilemma may be due to a potential emergency referral to hospital), or there may be difficult social issues.

When dealing with the case it is important to get some background. You need to find out the social situation, and ascertain exactly why a home visit was needed. Once you have done this try to determine what you think is wrong as you usually would. Make sure you spend a good amount of time on red flags, make sure the patient is safe at home.

If the patient is acutely unwell and you feel admission is needed, make sure you have explored any barriers to admission; this may be the crux of the case.

Make sure you know what your local arrangements for emergency home care are. If you have a complex social issue, you may need to be able to offer intermediate short term home help. This may be enough to allow an older or disabled person to remain at home when otherwise admission would be required. Make sure you talk the options through with the patient and uncover any fears they might have about coping.

Safety netting and follow up are again essential. Make sure the patient knows who to contact if the problem is not improving and what particular symptoms should lead them to do this.

Summary:

- Try not to be thrown by the change of scene

- Determine why a home visit was needed

- Ensure red flags are covered, make sure the patient doesn't need an emergency referral to hospital if they are unwell

- Think about short term extra care at home, and know what can be provided in your area

- Make sure you carefully safety net and arrange follow up

Third Party Consultations:

Just as in real life these can be extremely awkward. There are two reasons why you might be presented with one of these cases in the CSA. The most likely reason is that this is the most likely way that you will get a child case. Up until 2014 you could only get a child in this way; it is now possible to get child actors (but only over ten years old). The third party consultation is still a valid way for you to get a paediatric case. It is also a way for the examiners to test how you deal with a concerned relative.

In the paediatric third party consultation you are confronted usually with a parent who has not brought their child, but the consultation is about their child. To all intents and purposes this is a child health consultation, it's just that the child is not there so you don't need to interact with or examine them. Examining and interacting with a child is dealt with later in the paediatric chapter.

In this type of third party consultation it is highly unlikely that the child will be acutely unwell, but it is important you ensure that they are not, so ensure that when asking about red flags you do check regarding this as you have no opportunity to see or examine them. Make sure you listen to and take the carers concerns seriously. You may need to see the child, and it is perfectly appropriate that you defer giving a full diagnosis or final plan for now, just ensure that you explain why you need to see them, what it will add to the clinical picture, and what the carer could do meantime to help. It is likely the carer will be worried about their child, make sure that they leave with a better understanding of the situation and a reasonable plan as to what is going to happen next. You can also involve other healthcare professionals, for instance a paediatric nurse at the practice, the health visitor, school nurse, or local groups such as SureStart.

The other type of third party consultation involves an adult patient who is not present. There are many, many, reasons why they could put this into the exam. But in practice it is likely to be there in order to test how you deal with issues regarding confidentiality. Think about why the patient isn't there? Perhaps the patient doesn't know that the relative or carer has come to see you? Perhaps there are worries about dementia, violence, safety at home.

The key to this is to show the person who has come to see you that you are genuinely interested in helping the patient. Even if you can't tell them much because you don't have the patient's permission, you can still show them that you are interested and will take their worries on board.

It is very important that you do not tell a relative or carer anything personal about a patient unless it is expressly clear that you have the patient's permission to do so i.e. it is in the notes. If there is a confidentiality issue, explain it to the third party.

e.g. *'I know this might seem strange, but I cannot actually tell you much about X's condition. I know that you are his wife, but we do not actually know for sure that he is happy that I share his medical information with you. It is confidential. I can still listen to your concerns though, and I can do my best to help him. Perhaps if this is a problem your husband could contact the practice to give his permission, then in the future we could discuss these things more openly.'*

So here you have explained politely why you can't share certain info, but you have also covered an important additional point. Namely that you can still listen to her worries and help her. Confidentiality does not mean you can't take more info about a patient from someone; you simply can't give information about them, unless you are sure it is OK.

Assuming that the third party has come to you secretly because they are worried about the patient (a likely scenario), ensure that you get a good idea about the third party's worries, and also an understanding about what they are hoping you can do. You can arrange a reasonable plan. You may well need to see the patient and you may need to negotiate with the third party about how best to do this. Perhaps you can encourage them to share their concerns with the patient and bring them to see you?

Failing that, you may need to arrange a home visit, but ensure that you explain that you cannot force your help on the patient. You'll also need to agree with the carer how to avoid breaking *their* confidentiality. They may not want you to let the patient know certain things that they have told you. Make sure any sensitive information like this is discussed so that you would be better prepared to hypothetically see the patient in the future.

Summary:

- Ensure you don't break confidentiality

- Be very careful to ensure you take all concerns of the third party on board

- Be careful not to appear dismissive

- Explain your plan carefully and ensure the carer feels that it appropriately deals with their concerns

Learning difficulties:

This is another challenging case. Feedback generally is that the actors who do these stations are excellent, and it is very much like consulting a person with learning difficulties in real life.

When consulting someone with learning difficulties you can actually pretty much use your normal consultation structure. But the key is to remember that the patient may have difficulties in terms of understanding and retaining information. It is even more important in this station than any other to avoid jargon, even simple jargon such as: 'abdomen'—tummy.

Don't feel that you need to speak slower, and definitely do not be patronising; you simply need to use simpler language and make sure that you are clear. Take your time when taking the history. You might find it harder than usual to identify ideas, concerns, and expectations. Don't worry if the ideas, concerns, and expectations are not as expansive as usual, they may be simple requests e.g. 'I want the pain to stop'. The challenge here is likely to be accurately determining what is going on when you are unable to take as detailed a history as usual, and also negotiating a shared plan.

Particularly when making a plan or explaining, consider using shorter sentences than usual and checking understanding carefully as you go along.

Particularly ensure you take great care to explain why you need to examine the patient and what you are going to do. Look at the patient's face when you are examining; do not hurt them.

When you reach the end of the case make sure that you safety net very carefully. If the person has a carer who is not present you may also want to offer to contact this person on the patient's behalf to explain things.

Summary:

- Be careful not to be patronising

- Chunk and check more than you would do usually

- Avoid jargon, even simple jargon

- Be very careful when examining; do not make the patient afraid

- Carefully safety net using appropriate language and offer to contact a carer too if the patient wants

Paediatric case:

If you get one of the new child actors the current guidance is that the child will be over ten.

Ensure you introduce yourself to the child as well as to any carers who come with them. You want to make the child feel special—many children can be a bit frightened about coming to the doctor, take extra care to be non threatening.

To some extent these cases can be like third party consultations. You need to get the carers concerns on board but also ensure that you get the child's as well. With an older child you may wish to speak to them on their own for some of the case. The child may not wish this, or the carer may not allow it, but if it seems relevant to the case then feel free to offer this opportunity and explain why it might be useful. If no-one wants to do this then you could always leave it open as an option for the future.

I would usually introduce myself to the child first and direct my initial questions to the child, ensuring that I keep making eye contact with the carers now and again too. This can help gain the child's confidence and also will make you appear more confident speaking to children.

When it comes to examination of the child, explain carefully what you need to do, what exactly it entails, and why. If you think there could be some reluctance then you could always offer an illusory choice, for instance:

'Shall I listen to the front of your chest first or the back?'

This may make the child more comfortable and feel in control, but doesn't run the risk of a 'no' answer to whether you can examine them.

An older child may be able to have quite a lot of say in their treatment. Assuming they are 'Gillick competent', i.e. have capacity, then they are able to make treatment decisions without parental input. Regardless of whether they are Gillick competent, make sure you get the child's point of view as much as possible and involve them actively in discussions about the treatment options, taking theirs and their carer's views onboard to reach a decision which is hopefully acceptable to all and safe.

Summary:

- The child is the patient, make sure you keep them at the centre of the consultation

- Avoid being dismissive of the carer's concerns

- Consider offering the child some time to speak to you alone if this appears relevant in the case

- Make sure the child is as involved as they can be in decisions about their care

Psychiatric Case:

It is perfectly possible, in fact likely, that one of the cases that you will encounter in the exam will be psychiatric in nature. For many GPs and aspiring GPs a psychiatric case is something almost enjoyable – we can make a real difference to the patient just by talking to them. But for others it is the greatest test of their communication skills.

The key approach is to maintain patient focus whilst ensuring that the patient does not spend the whole ten minute appointment inappropriately offloading, or conversely become so withdrawn that they say little at all.

For the withdrawn patient, time needs to be spent developing a rapport; silence can be useful to an extent as well – thoughtful, considerate silence rather than threatening oppressing silence. If you ask a question and get no response why not wait just a few seconds longer than you normally would, with open body language and a calm, approachable expression, perhaps even a gentle nod. The patient may need a little longer to compose themselves before speaking. Perhaps they have something to tell you that they have never told anyone else? Perhaps they are suicidal and need to get up the courage to tell you.

For the rather garrulous patient it is sometimes necessary to interrupt. This needs to be done very gently – the patient is likely saying so much because they are deeply upset or anxious and feel they can confide in you. The truth is that offloading is extremely beneficial for the patient but it should ideally be done in a more controlled and longer environment (such as a CBT session with a trained therapist). If the patient offloads to you this will take up too much of the consultation, and you may not be best person to take on their problems and help them make sense of them. At this initial appointment your main aim is to encourage the patient to give you a full history, determine the level of risk, and make an initial management plan. Therapy may well be part of this plan, and the consultation should be empathetic and kind, but you need to ensure you cover the history and risk aspects too.

In terms of risk, these are the questions that people often find most difficult. There is something very hard about asking someone whether they are planning on ending their life. Signposting is once again your friend here. A simple phrase such as: 'Sometimes when people feel this depressed/anxious, they can start to have dark thoughts. Sometimes even thoughts of hurting or killing themselves. Have you ever had thoughts like this?'

Once you've assessed the patient it's time to move on to the management plan. For both depression and anxiety the research strongly points towards CBT type therapy being more beneficial than medication for most patients – especially in more mild cases. Most patients tend to have quite strong feelings about medication, either being very against it or being extremely keen to have it regardless of whether this is appropriate or not. It's important to try to establish the patients expectations first of course. Many patients do not wish to try psychological therapy, even though it may be the best treatment for them (either on its own or alongside medication in more severe anxiety or depression). This is often due to misconceptions about the therapy, concerns about talking to others, or stigma. It's often helpful in this situation to explain what CBT is,

e.g. 'don't worry, they're not going to make you lie on a couch and talk about your childhood! This is about finding links between thoughts you have, feelings they cause, and actions that you do because of them. Then the therapist helps you find ways to change the links so you can react differently.'

This makes it very clear that this isn't just about them having to talk about their problems, it's actually a targeted therapy. A targeted therapy that is often better than medication.

It's worth being prepared for a memory case as well. The approach would be the same, but the risks may be different. You should try to identify any risks at home (e.g. any instances where gas has been left on, and gauge how well the patient can look after themselves and what support they have), and also whether or not there is a risk regarding driving. If you are concerned about this, you should ask the patient not to drive until the outcome of any referral is known. Many patients with early dementia can drive safely though, so this needs to be carefully considered depending on the risks demonstrated. Probably the most important thing to remember here is to ensure you have saved in your memory some form of cognitive assessment. The GPCOG is probably the shortest reasonable one and can easily fit into about 4 minutes of the consult. If you have a memory case you will be expected to formally test the patient's memory during the consultation assuming the patient consents.

One of the most important aspects of the psychiatric case is ensuring follow up. This is important in terms of managing risk, but also it shows the patient that you are interested in their progress. Regardless of whether you start medication or not, or refer for psychological therapy or not, some form of follow up is almost always appropriate. If this is a new presentation of psychiatric illness blood tests are usually worth obtaining too, as many psychiatric illnesses can actually be mimicked by physical illnesses such as thyroid disease. These could be obtained between this appointment and the follow up appointment. A safety net is crucial as well, ensuring that you safety net for the possibility of worsening risk, so that the patient knows they can contact the surgery in an emergency if need be. If starting medication you should also cover the most common side effects and explain that no medication is likely to work for at least two weeks. This way the patient will have more realistic expectations of the treatment.

Summary:

- Stay patient centred, but ensure that the patient does not spend too much of the consultation offloading

- Good rapport early is essential, spend time and use silence as needed for the more withdrawn patient along with positive body language

- Do not be embarrassed to ask about risk. It is your job and signposting makes it easier

- Be ready to talk about the pros and cons of different treatments so the patient can make an informed choice

Practicalities of the CSA

Introduction:

'The only thing we have to fear is fear itself'

Franklin Roosevelt, 1933

This is an awful quote because it is quite plainly wrong. As Rimmer is keen to point out in the comedy show, 'Red Dwarf', we have far more to fear than just fear:

'We have nothing to fear but fear itself. Apart from pain. And maybe humiliation and obviously death. And failure. But apart from fear, pain and humiliation, failure, and the unknown, and death, we have nothing to fear but fear itself.'

Red Dwarf series 10 episode 6.

But perhaps the CSA is a case where if not the only thing we should fear is fear, then perhaps the *greatest* thing to fear, is fear. You see, if you can somehow not be absolutely terrified by the CSA then you are going to do an awful lot better, simply because you will be more natural. That is one of the major things they are looking for. They want to see you consult fluidly, conversationally. Fear makes this more difficult. So we need to look at ways of reducing fear and anxiety.

Don't get me wrong. It's completely natural and understandable to be worried about this exam, and unavoidable really. Everyone there is. It costs a fortune and you can easily mess it up. I was given similar advice: 'don't be frightened', by several of the registrars in the year above me and it annoyed me, so I am aware that telling you it will probably annoy you (for which I apologise!). It seems impossible to avoid fear. So rather than avoid it, let's look at how we can reduce it.

The reason I mention trying not to be scared, despite the annoyance it causes, is that if you can consult *naturally* you are far more likely to pass. Remember taking your driving test; the examiners are far more likely to pass a driver who is chatting to them, driving using his cerebellum mainly and looks like he has clocked up several hundred hours behind the wheel, rather than someone who is technically 'OK' but looks tense and is unable to speak to them because he is having to concentrate so hard on the road ahead.

The two keys to achieving the relaxed state needed are: consciously trying not to worry, and practice. I found that the best way of not worrying too much was to purposely try to see the exam as a mock, (albeit a hideously expensive one). I took the exam at the earliest opportunity in ST3, November, (our scheme starts October to October), so that I could resit in May when I failed it. As a result I was much less stressed about my November sitting as I went in almost resigned to the fact that I was taking it too early, and should therefore not pass it. I was very pleasantly surprised to find that I did not have to resit in May despite expecting a high possibility of failure.

Try to find some trick that works for you. But most importantly—practice. Familiarity, as they say, breeds contempt (or at least confidence). How to practice? I will cover below.

The Run up to the Exam:

"This is the real secret of life—to be completely engaged with what you are doing in the here and now; and instead of calling it work: realise it is play."

Alan Watts

To most effectively practice you might think that all you need do is see a lot of patients. This would be true if the exam was indeed a complete simulation of UK general practice. I don't want to be hard on the exam, which I generally think is quite good, but ultimately its greatest problem is that, like any exam, it is not a perfect test of what it purports to be testing. It tests whether you are ready to be GP by using a surrogate measure: How well can you consult an actor, whilst being watched by an examiner, in a strange room in London.

Don't get hung up on this, simply use this understanding to help you practice more effectively.

Please don't misunderstand me here, I'm not saying there is no point seeing lots of patients. Of course you need to do this; you are training to be a GP. But, please don't fall into the trap of thinking that doing this will guarantee you a pass. Also don't fall into the easy trap of just revising knowledge because this is the 'easy' thing to do. You need the working knowledge of a GP to pass this exam, but do not make the mistake of considering this exam a knowledge test—why else would they have the AKT?

If you want to reduce anxiety by fully preparing for the exam you need to practice the actual situation that the exam tests. You are going to have to role play. You are going to have to get a group going, meet regularly, practice and be ruthless. It sounds hard and it will probably be a bit embarrassing at times as you watch each other consult, but it will be worth it when you pass. It's also a very fast way to get feedback and improve your consultation skills and communication skills.

When you get a study group together, try to make sure it comprises both overseas trainees and British trainees, you can both learn a lot from each other. You need to meet regularly, even if it's just once a week. Decide in advance that you will take this commitment seriously, and as well as talking about life a bit, that you will do many cases each time you meet. I would recommend meeting at least weekly for six months, for at least 3 hours each time. Whilst you are there, discuss the 'tools' in this book and think about how to apply them and any problems you have had whilst applying them. Hone the skills till they suit you. Remember this is about developing your own toolkit of skills, not mine. Your natural consultation will not be exactly like mine—that is the beauty of it. If it was exactly like mine you would be formulaic and you would be marked down for it and not be able to react to the evolving consultation. You need to practice to become completely fluid in your use of these skills.

To practice I would recommend buying some books full of cases for role play, there are several books like this available easily in shops and online. Personally I steered clear of the ones that just had clinical scenarios and lists of what to do, there are much more useful (in my opinion) books which contain thirty odd cases, each with a 'candidate information', 'role player information' and a 'what you should have done' page. Although these are not necessarily going to be completely similar to the cases in the CSA, they will still allow you to practice your skills.

My most important tip is to be ruthless with each other in your small groups. You *have* to tell someone if you don't like the way they are doing something in the consultation. It feels horrible to point it out, but if you don't they won't know and they might carry that habit into the CSA. Agree to be ruthless with each other and the sessions will be far more useful.

In the last two weeks try to rope friends who are not GP regs in as well. They can do role playing, and will be even better at it if they are non medics as who won't subconsciously help you. Try to run a mock CSA if you can get enough volunteers. Run it to time to try to get a feel of what doing 13 cases one after another feels like.

Keeping a clear mind:

I want to know why is everyone against me. I want to know what has happened to my friends. Why do I feel like the world is against me? Am I really on my own?

'Fight your Demons', from 'Vol 5. Lost at Home', by 'More than a Thousand'

There is, as I'm sure that you are aware, an ongoing debate about the fairness of the CSA—most importantly as to whether the exam is biased against trainees who trained outside the UK. There are even websites and books that give practical advice on how to avoid this.

Clearly there is an ongoing investigation into this, and certainly if bias is truly shown then it is paramount that the college does anything it can to stop this. Meanwhile you are in situation where you need to take the exam anyway and make the best of it.

My one piece of advice here is to try to shut these worries out as much as possible. Look back over this book. The examiners want to see you consult naturally, like a conversation; they don't want to see you acting. If you spend the six months in the run up to the exam focusing on changing your voice, appearance, dress, mannerisms etc, into what someone else thinks the examiner is looking for, then how do you expect to consult naturally?

If you trained abroad then please do throw yourself into local activities where you live and soak up local culture, this will be fun and teach you more about the UK and may help you consult British people more easily. But please don't try to change who you are, no matter what anyone else tells you. The best hope that any of us have for passing this exam first time is to try to stay calm and consult naturally, so that the consultation flows like a conservation guided by your skill and the patient's problems. You want your 'inner voice' to be telling you about the body language of the patient, not paying attention to whether you are speaking in the way you were told the examiners like.

Travel:

Unless you actually live in London try to come up the day before. London is huge and you'll be far less stressed if you have done a quick reconnoiter of the building the day before. No last minute panic.

The day before, try to do some sightseeing, go to a show, have a drink somewhere nice, just anything to not think too much about why you are there. It's really important to remember again that knowledge cannot save you now. You know enough, your skills are honed through your practice groups. There is no point trying to revise the day before this exam like you could for your AKT, it is simply not crammable. Try to enjoy yourself.

The Day Itself:

Once more into the fray. Into the last good fight I'll ever know. Live and die on this day. Live and die on this day.

Ottway - The Grey

Arrive early. They say you need to be there by 9 for a morning start, get there at quarter to, you'll be less stressed. I arrived fifteen minutes early but was one of the last to get there. You'll be ushered into a lift and let out into a room where you will hand in your possessions (show your passport etc), and be given an identity badge to wear around your neck. You will then be ushered into a small side room where you will sit in awkward silence with many people you don't know. Many of them will be reading their BNFs, but you know that this won't help you now, so don't do it. Try to talk to someone. If no-one wants to talk just think about what you are going to be doing after the exam. Plan a pub crawl based on a tube line if you like; just whatever you do, don't think too hard about the exam that is coming.

After what seems like ages the lead examiner will come in and demo the alarms that go off at the end of each case. You will then be led to your 'stream'. The colour of your badge will identify you to a particular stream who will all face the same patients that session. You will then put your bag into a locker and put all of your doctor equipment into a clear bag they give you. Finally they will let you into your room where, apparently, they give you fifteen minutes to get set up. This fifteen minutes seems to go in about five so make full use of it. Feel free to move the furniture so that it's like your ideal consultation room. Set up the equipment so that you feel at home, and have a look at the special gear they leave lying around on the desk. They give you extra equipment that might (or might not) be relevant to the cases such as a neurotip, tuning fork, gestation calculators etc. So if any of it is new to you, have a play so that you can seem practiced when it comes to using it for real.

You want to spend as much of the fifteen minutes as you can actually reading the cases. Try to get through all fifteen if you can, but if you are pressed for time just get through as many as you can. Don't worry excessively about what you read in a later patient's notes and the problems that might be coming—simply be aware, you are just gathering information for later.

Notice above you that there is a clock, this resets when the patient walks in and counts upwards to 10.

When the prep time is up the lead examiner will ask if all the actors and examiners are ready, and then...

The first buzzer will go off...

The actor will knock on the door....

Get up, and go and greet them with a handshake.

Good luck.

And remember the great words of Zefram Cochrane:

'Don't try to be a great man. Just be a man, and let history make its own judgment.'

Star Trek First Contact

References

I have specifically with this book, aimed to not quote much from other sources. I wanted this book to be my personal opinion on a range of consultation related subjects, not to be a rehash of other people's books. However, many of the skills I have learnt I have learnt from these sources below.

Where I have relied on a book for a point made in the book, I have directly referenced it within the text by number.

For further consultation skills training may I recommend all of the below.

1. *The Naked Consultation - a practical guide to primary care consultation skills* - Liz Moulton
2. RCGP website
3. *'The Inner Consultation', how to develop an effective and intuitive consultation style'* - Neighbour
4. *A General Theory Of Love* - Lewis, Amini, Lannon
5. *Watching The English - The hidden rules of English Behaviour* - Kate Fox
6. *Meetings Between Experts: An Approach to Sharing Ideas in Medical Consultations* – Tuckett
7. http://www.nlpls.com/articles/perceptualPositions.php

8. http://www.gmc-uk.org/static/documents/content/Consent_-_English_0911.pdf
9. *I Don't Know What it is But I Don't Think it's Serious: Confidence and Decisiveness in Primary Care* – Tim Crossley
10. http://www.nice.org.uk/nicemedia/pdf/CG47NICEGuideline.pdf

About the Author

Dan Berkeley lives with his wife and three children in Cumbria, near to the edge of the Lake District. He is a GP at Maryport group practice by the sea, and also BBC radio Cumbria's resident radio doctor. He started writing nine years ago, but had the idea for his first novel, 'Sacramentum', five years before that whilst awaking from a barely remembered dream. He has been interested in ancient history since he was a child, but was fairly useless at Latin whilst at school. Unfortunately he thought that to do medicine you needed A levels all in sciences, and so didn't do classical civilisation as a subject past GCSE. He therefore spent most of his time at medical school reading books about ancient Rome and Greece, and drinking ale. Whilst at school he did try writing some short stories, but with no exceptions—these were awful. Even his English teacher told him they were awful. Having read every ancient history book in the library, and enjoying the works of Bernard Cornwell, Conn Iggulden, Wilbur Smith, and Robert Harris, he felt it was time to try to combine three ideas: write an alternative history in the style of 'Fatherland', with the type of action and characterisation of an Iggulden or Cornwell novel, and the sickening descriptive brutality of a Smith book. At least he was writing what he wanted to read. The result was 'Sacramentum', and two years later its better sequels, 'Impietas' and 'Ultionis'.

When he is not writing he also enjoys: strategic board gaming, medicine, brewing ale, drumming (badly), walking on the fells, and trying to eat as many different types of animal as possible. This is his first nonfiction book.

Printed by Amazon Italia Logistica S.r.l.
Torrazza Piemonte (TO), Italy